K

BOOKS BY ROBERT PENN WARREN

John Brown: The Making of a Martyr

Thirty-six Poems

Night Rider

Eleven Poems on the Same Theme

At Heaven's Gate

Selected Poems, 1923–1943

All the King's Men

Blackberry Winter

The Circus in the Attic

World Enough and Time

Brother to Dragons

Band of Angels

Segregation: The Inner Conflict in the South

Promises: Poems 1954–1956

Selected Essays

The Cave

All the King's Men (play)

You, Emperors, and Others: Poems 1957–1960

The Legacy of the Civil War

Wilderness

Flood

Who Speaks for the Negro?

Selected Poems: New and Old 1923–1966

Incarnations: Poems 1966–1968

Audubon: A Vision

Homage to Theodore Dreiser

Meet Me in the Green Glen

Or Else—Poem/Poems 1968–1974

OR ELSE–
Poem / Poems 1968—1974

⌒Robert Penn Warren

OR ELSE~
Poem/Poems 1968-1974

RANDOM HOUSE NEW YORK

811
W

All rights reserved under International and Pan-American
Copyright Conventions. Published in the United States by
Random House, Inc., New York, and simultaneously in
Canada by Random House of Canada Limited, Toronto.

Some of these poems originally appeared in *The Atlantic Monthly,*
Esquire, Yale Review, The New York Review of Books, The New Yorker,
Salmagundi, The Southern Review, Harper's, Yale Literary Magazine,
The Sou'wester, and *I. A. Richards: Essays in His Honor,* edited by Reuben Brower,
Helen Vendler, and John Hollander (Oxford University Press, 1973).

Poems from Robert Penn Warren's *Selected Poems, New and Old 1923–1966,*
Incarnations and *Homage to Theodore Dreiser* all used by
permission of Random House, Inc.

Library of Congress Cataloging in Publication Data

Warren, Robert Penn, 1905–   Or else—poem/poems 1968–1974.

    I. Title.
PS3545.A74807   1974   811'.5'2   74-9055
ISBN 0-394-49448-2
ISBN 0-394-49501-2 (limited edition)

Manufactured in the United States of America

98765432

FIRST EDITION

TO CESARE AND RYSIA LOMBROSO

CONTENTS

I   The Nature of a Mirror   3
    Interjection # 1: The Need for Re-evaluation   4

II   Natural History   5

III   Time as Hypnosis   7

IV   Blow, West Wind   10
    Interjection # 2: Caveat   11

V   I Am Dreaming of a White Christmas: The Natural
    History of a Vision   13
    Interjection # 3: I Know a Place Where All Is Real   23

VI   Ballad of Mister Dutcher and the Last Lynching in Gupton   25

VII   Chain Saw at Dawn in Vermont in Time of Drouth   30

VIII   Small White House   34
    Interjection # 4: Bad Year, Bad War: a New Year's Card, 1969   35

IX   Forever O'clock   37

X   Rattlesnake Country   40

XI   Homage to Theodore Dreiser   49
    1. Psychological Profile   49
    2. Vital Statistics   51
    3. Moral Assessment   54

XII   Flaubert in Egypt   55
    Interjection # 5: Solipsism and Theology   58

XIII   The True Nature of Time   59
    1. The Faring   59
    2. The Enclave   61

XIV   Vision Under the October Mountain: A Love Poem   62

XV   Stargazing   64
    Interjection # 6: What You Sometimes Feel on Your Face at Night   66

XVI   News Photo 67

XVII   Little Boy and Lost Shoe 74

XVIII   Composition in Gold and Red-Gold 75

       Interjection # 7: Remarks of Soul to Body 78

XIX   There's a Grandfather's Clock in the Hall 80

XX   Reading Late at Night, Thermometer Falling 82

XXI   Folly on Royal Street Before the Raw Face of God 90

       Interjection # 8: Or, Sometimes, Night 93

XXII   Sunset Walk in Thaw-Time in Vermont 94

XXIII   Birth of Love 98

XXIV   A Problem in Spatial Composition 101

This book is conceived as a single long poem composed
of a number of shorter poems as sections or chapters.
It is dated 1968–1974, but a few short pieces come
from a period some ten years before, when I was working
toward a similar long poem. After a time, however, I
was to find that that poem was distintegrating into a
miscellany, and so abandoned the project and published
the pieces that I wished to preserve under the title
"Notes on a Life to Be Lived." More lately, working on
this book, I have decided that all except three of those early
pieces have a place in the thematic structure of this poem.
For the same reason, I have here drawn another poem,
"The True Nature of Time," from a more recent volume.

R . P . W .

He clave the rocks in the wilderness, and gave them drink as out of the great depths.

Psalms, 78: 15

OR ELSE—
Poem/Poems 1968–1974

* This symbol is used to indicate a space between sections of a poem wherever such spaces are lost in pagination.

I ∽
THE NATURE OF A MIRROR

The sky has murder in the eye, and I
Have murder in the heart, for I
Am only human.
We look at each other, the sky and I.
We understand each other, for

The solstice of summer has sagged, I stand
And wait. Virtue is rewarded, that
Is the nightmare, and I must tell you

That soon now, even before
The change from Daylight Saving Time, the sun,
Beyond the western ridge of black-burnt pine stubs like
A snaggery of rotten shark teeth, sinks
Lower, larger, more blank, and redder than
A mother's rage, as though
F.D.R. had never run for office even, or the first vagina
Had not had the texture of dream. Time

Is the mirror into which you stare.

INTERJECTION #1:
THE NEED FOR RE-EVALUATION

Is this really me? Of course not, for Time
Is only a mirror in the fun-house.

You must re-evaluate the whole question.

In the rain the naked old father is dancing, he will get wet.
The rain is sparse, but he cannot dodge all the drops.

He is singing a song, but the language is strange to me.

The mother is counting her money like mad, in the sunshine.
Like shuttles her fingers fly, and the sum is clearly astronomical.

Her breath is sweet as bruised violets, and her smile sways like
daffodils reflected in a brook.

The song of the father tells how at last he understands.
That is why the language is strange to me.

That is why clocks all over the continent have stopped.

The money the naked old mother counts is her golden memories of love.
That is why I see nothing in her maniacally busy fingers.

That is why all flights have been canceled out of Kennedy.

✿

As much as I hate to, I must summon the police.
For their own good, as well as that of society, they
                                    must be put under surveillance.

They must learn to stay in their graves. That is what graves are for.

III ∽
TIME AS HYPNOSIS

For I. A. Richards

White, white in that dawnlight, the world was exploding, white
Light bursting from whiteness. What
Is the name of the world?—for

Whiteness, all night from the black sky unfeathering,
Had changed the world's name, and maybe
My own, or maybe it was all only
A dream I was having, but did not
Know it, or maybe the truth was that I,
Huddling tight in the blankets and darkness and self,
Was nothing, was nothing but what
The snow dreamed all night. Then light:

Two years and no snow in our section, and two years
Is a long time when you are twelve. So,

All day in a landscape that had been
Brown fields and black woods but was now
White emptiness and arches,
I wandered. The white light
Filled all the vertiginous sky, and even
My head until it
Spread bright and wide like another sky under which I

Wandered. I came
To a place where the woods were, stood under
A crazed geometry of boughs black but
Snow-laden and criss-crossed with light, and between
Banks of humped snow and whiteness of ice-fret, saw
Black water slide slow, and glossy as sleep.

I stared at the water, and staring, wondered
What the white-bellied minnow, now deep in
Black leaf-muck and mud, thought.
I thought of the muskrat dim in his mud-gloom.

Have you ever seen how delicately
Etched the print of the field mouse's foot in fresh snow is?
I saw the tracks. But suddenly, none. Nothing
But the wing-flurried snow. Then, small as a pin-head, the single
Bright-frozen, red bead of a blood-drop. Have you ever
Stared into the owl's eyes? They blink slow, then burn:
Burn gold in the dark inner core of the snow-shrouded cedar.

There was a great field that tilted
Its whiteness up to the line where the slant, blue knife-edge of sky
Cut it off. I stood
In the middle of that space. I looked back, saw
My own tracks march at me. Mercilessly,
They came at me and did not stop. Ahead,
Was the blankness of white. Up it rose. Then the sky.

Evening came, and I sat by the fire, and the flame danced.

✿

All day, I had wandered in the glittering metaphor
For which I could find no referent.

All night, that night, asleep, I would wander, lost in a dream
That was only what the snow dreamed.

IV 〜
BLOW, WEST WIND

I know, I know—though the evidence
Is lost, and the last who might speak are dead.
Blow, west wind, blow, and the evidence, O,

Is lost, and wind shakes the cedar, and O,
I know how the kestrel hung over Wyoming,
Breast reddened in sunset, and O, the cedar

Shakes, and I know how cold
Was the sweat on my father's mouth, dead.
Blow, west wind, blow, shake the cedar, I know

How once I, a boy, crouching at creekside,
Watched, in the sunlight, a handful of water
Drip, drip, from my hand. The drops—they were bright!

But you believe nothing, with the evidence lost.

INTERJECTION #2:
CAVEAT

For John Crowe Ransom

Necessarily, we must think of the
world as continuous, for if it were
not so I would have told you, for I have
bled for this knowledge, and every man
is a sort of Jesus, but in any
case, if it were not so, you wouldn't know
you are in the world, or even that the
world exists at all—

          but only, oh, on-
ly, in discontinuity, do we
know that we exist, or that, in the deep-
est sense, the existence of anything
signifies more than the fact that it is
continuous with the world.

            A new high-
way is under construction. Crushed rock has
been spread for miles and rolled down. On Sunday,
when no one is there, go and stand on the
roadbed. It stretches before your eyes in-
to distance. But fix your eyes firmly on
one fragment of crushed rock. Now, it only

glows a little, inconspicuously
one might say. But soon, you will notice a
slight glittering. Then a marked vibration
sets in. You brush your hand across your eyes,
but, suddenly, the earth underfoot is
twitching. Then, remarkably, the bright sun
jerks like a spastic, and all things seem to
be spinning away from the univer-
sal center that the single fragment of
crushed rock has ineluctably become.

At this point, while there is still time and will,
I advise you to detach your gaze from
that fragment of rock. Not all witnesses
of the phenomenon survive unchanged
the moment when, at last, the object screams

in an ecstasy of

being.

V 〜

I AM DREAMING OF A WHITE CHRISTMAS:
THE NATURAL HISTORY OF A VISION

For Andrew Vincent Corry

[1]

No, not that door,—never! But,
Entering, saw. Through
Air brown as an old daguerreotype fading. Through
Air that, though dust to the tongue, yet—
Like the inward, brown-glimmering twilight of water—
Swayed. Through brown air, dust-dry, saw. Saw
It.

    The bed.

         Where it had
Been. Now was. Of all
Covering stripped, the mattress
Bare but for old newspapers spread.
Curled edges. Yellow. On yellow paper dust,
The dust yellow. No! Do not.

            Do not lean to
Look at that date. Do not touch
That silken and yellow perfection of Time that
Dust is, for
There is no Time. I,
Entering, see.

✿

I,
Standing here, breathe the dry air.

[2]
See
Yonder the old Morris chair bought soon
After marriage, for him to rest after work in, the leather,
Once black, now browning, brown at the dry cracks, streaked
With a fungoid green. Approaching,
See.

See it.

The big head. Propped,
Erect on the chair's leather pillow, bald skin
Tight on skull, not white now, brown
Like old leather lacquered, the big nose
Brown-lacquered, bold-jutting yet but with
Nostril-flanges gone tattered in Time. I have not
Yet looked at the eyes. Not
Yet.

The eyes
Are not there. But,
Not there, they stare at what
Is not there.

[3]
Not there, but
In each of the appropriate twin apertures, which are
Deep and dark as a thumb-gouge,

Something that might be taken for
A mulberry, large and black-ripe when, long back, crushed,
But now, with years, dust-dried. The mulberries,
Crushed and desiccated, each out of
Its dark lurking-place, stare out at
Nothing.

       His eyes
Had been blue.

[4]
        Hers brown. But
Are not now. Now staring,
She sits in the accustomed rocker, but with
No motion. I cannot
Be sure what color the dress once was, but
Am sure that the fabric now falls decisively away
From the Time-sharpened angle of knees. The fabric
Over one knee, the left, has given way. And
I see what protrudes.

       See it.

       Above,
The dry fabric droops over breastlessness.

Over the shrouded femurs that now are the lap, the hands,
Palm-down, lie. The nail of one forefinger
Is missing.

      On the ring-finger of the left hand
There are two diamond rings. On that of the right,

One. On Sundays, and some evenings
When she sat with him, the diamonds would be on the fingers.

The rings. They shone.

Shine now.

In the brown air.

On the brown-lacquered face
There are now no
Lips to kiss with.

[5]
The eyes had been brown. But
Now are not where eyes had been. What things
Now are where eyes had been but
Now are not, stare. At the place where now
Is not what once they
Had stared at.

There is no fire on the cold hearth now,
To stare at.

[6]
        On
The ashes, gray, a piece of torn orange peel.
Foil wrappings of chocolates, silver and crimson and gold,
Yet gleaming from grayness. Torn Christmas paper,
Stamped green and red, holly and berries, not
Yet entirely consumed, but warped

And black-gnawed at edges. I feel
Nothing. A red
Ribbon, ripped long ago from some package of joy,
Winds over the gray hearth like
A fuse that failed. I feel
Nothing.

       Not even
When I see the tree.

Why had I not seen the tree before?
Why, on entering, had I not seen it?
It must have been there, and for
A long time, for
The boughs are, of all green, long since denuded.
That much is clear. For the floor
Is there carpeted thick with the brown detritus of cedar.

Christmas trees in our section always were cedar.

[7]
Beneath the un-greened and brown-spiked tree,
On the dead-fall of brown frond-needles, are,
I see, three packages. Identical in size and shape.
In bright Christmas paper. Each with red bow, and under
The ribbon, a sprig of holly.

       But look!

          The holly

Is, clearly, fresh.

❁

I say to myself:

The holly is fresh.

And
My breath comes short. For I am wondering
Which package is mine.

Oh, which?

I have stepped across the hearth and my hand stretches out.

But the voice:

No presents, son, till the little ones come.

[8]
What shadow of tongue, years back unfleshed, in what
Darkness locked in a rigid jaw, can lift and flex?

The man and the woman sit rigid. What had been
Eyes stare at the cold hearth, but I
Stare at the three chairs. Why—
Tell me why—had I not observed them before? For
They are here.

The little red chair,
For the baby. The next biggest chair
For my little sister, the little red rocker. Then,
The biggest, my own, me the eldest.

The chairs are all empty.

✳

                    But
I am thinking a thought that is louder than words.
Thinking:

          They're empty, they're empty, but me—oh, I'm here!

And that thought is not words, but a roar like wind, or
The roar of the night-freight beating the rails of the trestle,
And you under the trestle, and the roar
Is nothing but darkness alive. Suddenly,
Silence.

          And no
Breath comes.

[9]
                    Where I was,
Am not. Now am
Where the blunt crowd thrusts, nudges, jerks, jostles,
And the eye is inimical. Then,
Of a sudden, know:

                    Times Square, the season
Late summer and the hour sunset, with fumes
In throat and smog-glitter at sky-height, where
A jet, silver and ectoplasmic, spooks through
The sustaining light, which
Is yellow as acid. Sweat,
Cold in arm-pit, slides down flesh.

The flesh is mine.

✿

What year it is, I can't, for the life of me,
Guess, but know that,
Far off, south-eastward, in Bellevue,
In a bare room with windows barred, a woman,
Supine on an iron cot, legs spread, each ankle
Shackled to the cot-frame,
Screams.

She keeps on screaming because it is sunset.

Her hair has been hacked short.

[10]
Clerks now go home, night watchmen wake up, and the heart
Of the taxi-driver, just coming on shift,
Leaps with hope.

All is not in vain.

Old men come out from the hard-core movies.
They wish they had waited till later.

They stand on the pavement and stare up at the sky.
Their drawers are drying stiff at the crotch, and
The sky dies wide. The sky
Is far above the first hysteria of neon.

Soon they will want to go and get something to eat.

Meanwhile, down the big sluice of Broadway,
The steel logs jerk and plunge
Until caught in the rip, snarl, and eddy here before my face.

✿

A mounted policeman sits a bay gelding. The rump
Of the animal gleams expensively. The policeman
Is some sort of dago. His jowls are swart.
His eyes are bright with seeing.

He is as beautiful as a law of chemistry.

[11]
In any case,
I stand here and think of snow falling. But am
Not here. Am
Otherwhere, for already,
This early and summer not over, in West Montana—
Or is it Idaho?—in
The Nez Percé Pass, tonight
It will be snowing.

The Nez Percé is more than 7,000 feet, and I
Have been there. The first flakes,
Large, soft, sparse, come straight down
And with enormous deliberation, white
Out of unbreathing blackness. Snow
Does not yet cling, but the tall stalk of bear-grass
Is pale in darkness. I have seen, long ago,
The paleness of bear-grass in darkness.

                              But tell me, tell me,
Will I never know
What present there was in that package for me,
Under the Christmas tree?

✿

[12]

All items listed above belong in the world
In which all things are continuous,
And are parts of the original dream which
I am now trying to discover the logic of. This
Is the process whereby pain of the past in its pastness
May be converted into the future tense

Of joy.

INTERJECTION #3:
I KNOW A PLACE WHERE ALL IS REAL

For Austin Warren

I know a place where all is real. I
have been there, therefore
know. Access is not easy, the way
rough, and visibility extremely poor, especially
among the mountains. Maps
show only the blank space, somewhere
northwest of Mania and beyond Delight,
but if you can manage to elude the natives of
intervening zones, who practice
ghastly rites and have an appetite for human flesh,
you may find a sly track through
narrow and fog-laced passes. Meanwhile
give little credence to tales told
by returning travelers or those
who pretend to be such. But truth,
sometimes, is even more unacceptable
to the casual hearer, and in bars
I have been laughed at for reporting
the simple facts.

        In any case,
few travelers do return.
Among those who choose to remain and apply

for naturalization, a certain number
find that they cannot stand the altitude, but these,
upon making their way out, sometimes die of an oppressive
pulmonary complaint as soon as they hit the low country.

BALLAD OF MISTER DUTCHER
AND THE LAST LYNCHING IN GUPTON

He must have been just as old in
days when young as later, his face
as gray and his eyes not gray but
that color there's not even a
name for—all this the same as when,
years later, he'd walk down the street,
and I, a boy, would then see him
in his worn-out gray coat going
twice a day to the depot, where
he'd handle what express came, then
twice a day going back home, the
first time to eat, the last to shut
the door of his small gray house, and
not be seen till tomorrow, and
if ever you said hello, he
might say whatever it was that
you never quite caught, but always
his face had a sort of gray smile
turned more inside than out, as though
there was something he knew but knew
that you'd never know what it was he knew.

He had a small wife whose face was

as gray as the gingham she wore,
or the gray coat that on Sunday
she wore to church, and nobody
could ever imagine what, in
that small gray house, those gray faces
might ever say to each other,
or think, as they lay side by side
while his eyes of that color you
couldn't ever name stared up where
dark hid the ceiling. But we knew
how he'd smile in the dark who knew
that he knew what we'd never know he knew.

But time brings all things to light, so
long after the gray-faced wife was
dead, and the hump of her grave sunk
down to a trench, and the one gray-
faced son dead to boot, having died
one cold winter night in jail, where
the town constable had put him
to sober up—well, long after,
being left all alone with his
knowledge of what we'd never know he knew,

he, in the fullness of time, and
in glory, brought it forth. One hot
afternoon in Hoptown, some fool
nigger, wall-eyed drunk and with a
four-bit hand-gun, tried to stick up
a liquor store, shot the clerk, and,
still broke, grabbed a freight, and was high-
tailing for Gupton, in happy
ignorance that the telephone

had ever been invented. So
when they flagged down the freight, the fool
nigger made one more mistake, up
and drilled one of the posse. That
was that, and in five minutes he
was on his way to the county
seat, the constable driving, but
mighty slow, while back there
in Gupton, in the hardware store,
a business transaction concern-
ing rope was in due process. It
was the small gray-faced man who, to
general astonishment though
in a low, gray voice, said: "Gimme
that rope." Quick as a wink, six turns
around the leader, the end snubbed,
and there was that neat cylinder
of rope the noose line could slide through
easy as a greased piston or
the dose of salts through the widow-
woman, and that was what Mister
Dutcher, all the days, weeks, and years,
had known, and nobody'd known that he knew.

The constable, it sort of seemed,
had car trouble, and there he was
by the road, in the cooling shade
of a big white oak, with his head
stuck under the hood and a wrench
in his hand. They grabbed him before
he even got his head out, which,
you could tell, was not in any
great hurry anyway. Well, what

happened was not Mister Dutcher's
fault, nor the rope's, it was only
that that fool nigger just would not
cooperate, for when the big
bread truck they had him standing on
drew out, he hung on with both feet
as long as possible, then just
keeled over, slow and head-down, in-
to the rope, spilling his yell out
like five gallons of fresh water
in one big, bright, out-busting slosh
in the sunshine, if you, of a
sudden, heave over the crock. So,
that fool nigger managed never
to get a good, clean drop, which was,
you might say, his last mistake. One
man started vomiting, but one
put six .44's in, and that
quieted down the main performer.
Well, that was how we came to know
what Mister Dutcher'd thought we'd never know.

But isn't a man entitled
to something he can call truly
his own—even to his pride in
that one talent kept, against the
advice of Jesus, wrapped in a
napkin, and death to hide? Any-
way, what does it matter now, for
Mister Dutcher is not there to
walk the same old round like a blind
mule hitched to a sorghum mill, is,
in fact, in some nook, niche, crack or

cubby of eternity, stowed
snug as a bug, and safe from all
contumely, wrath, hurt ego, and
biologic despair, with no
drop of his blood to persist in
that howling orthodoxy of
darkness that, like speed-hurled rain on
glass, streams past us, and is Time. At
all events, I'm the one man left
who has any reason at all
to remember his name, and if
truth be told, I haven't got so
damned much, but some time, going back,
I might try to locate the stone
it's on, if grass and ragweed aren't too high.

I might even try to locate
where that black man got buried, though
that would, of course, be somewhat difficult.

VII〜
CHAIN SAW AT DAWN IN VERMONT
IN TIME OF DROUTH

1.

Dawn and, distant, the steel-snarl and lyric
Of the chain saw in deep woods:
I wake. Was it
Trunk-scream, bough-rip and swish, then earth-thud?
No—only the saw's song, the saw
Sings: *now!* Sings:
Now, now, now, in the
Lash and blood-lust of an eternal present, the present
Murders the past, the nerve shrieks, the saw

Sings *now,* and I wake, rising
From that darkness of sleep which
Is the past, and is
The self. It is
Myself, and I know how,
Now far off,
New light gilds the spruce-tops.
The saw, for a moment, ceases, and under
Arm-pits of the blue-shirted sawyer sweat
Beads cold, and
In the obscene silence of the saw's cessation,
A crow, somewhere, calls.

❈

The crow, in distance, calls with the crystalline beauty
Of the outraged heart.

Have I learned how to live?

2.

On the other side of the woods, in the village, a man
Is dying. Wakes
In dawn to the saw's song, thinks
How his wife was a good wife, wonders
Why his boy turned out bad, wonders why
He himself never managed to pay off the mortgage, thinks
Of dawn and the first light spangling the spruces, and how
He leaned on the saw and the saw
Sang. But had not known what
The saw sang. So now thinks:
I have not learned how to die, but

For that thought has no language, has only
The saw's song, in distance: glee of steel and the
Sun-shriek, the scream of castration, the whirl-tooth hysteria
Of *now, now, now!* So
Sweats. What

Can I tell him? I
Cannot tell him how to die because
I have not learned how to live—what man
Has learned how to live?—and I lie

In the dawn, and the thin sheet of summer
Lies on me, and I close my eyes, for
The saw sings, and I know
That soon I must rise and go out in the world where
The heel of the sun's foot smites horridly the hill,
And the stalk of the beech leaf goes limp,
And the bright brook goes gray among boulders,
And the saw sings, for

✿

I must endeavor to learn what
I must learn before I must learn
The other thing. If
I learn even a little, I may,
By evening, be able
To tell the man something.

Or he himself may have learned by then.

VIII ∽
SMALL WHITE HOUSE

The sun of July beats down on the small white house.
The pasture is brown-bright as brass, and like brass, sings with heat.
Halt! And I stand here, hills shudder, withdraw into distance,
Leprous with light. And a child's cry comes from the house.

Tell me, oh, where, in what state, did I see the small white house,
Which I see in my mind?—And the wax-wing's beak slices the blue cedar-berry,
Which is as blue as distance. The river, far off, shrinks
Among the hot boulders, no glister, looks dead as a discarded snake-skin
                                        rubbed off on stone. The house

Swims in that dazzle of no-Time. The child's cry comes from the house.

INTERJECTION #4:
BAD YEAR, BAD WAR:
A NEW YEAR'S CARD, 1969

> *And almost all things are by the law purged*
> *with blood; and without shedding of blood*
> *there is no remission.*
>
> Epistle to the Hebrews, 9:22.

That was the year of the bad war. The others—
Wars, that is—had been virtuous. If blood

Was shed, it was, in a way, sacramental, redeeming
Even evil enemies from whose veins it flowed,

Into the benign logic of History; and some,
By common report even the most brutalized, died with a shy

And grateful smile on the face, as though they,
At the last, understood. Our own wounds were, of course, precious.

There is always imprecision in human affairs, and war
Is not exception, therefore the innocent—

Though innocence is, it should be remembered, a complex concept—
Must sometimes suffer. There is the blunt

Justice of the falling beam, the paw-flick of
The unselective flame. But happily,

If one's conscience attests to ultimate innocence,
Then the brief suffering of others, whose innocence is only incidental,

✿

Can be regarded, with pity to be sure, as merely
The historical cost of the process by which

The larger innocence fulfills itself in
The realm of contingency. For conscience

Is, of innocence, the final criterion, and the fact that now we
Are troubled, and candidly admit it, simply proves

That in the past we, being then untroubled,
Were innocent. Dear God, we pray

To be restored to that purity of heart
That sanctifies the shedding of blood.

IX ∽
FOREVER O'CLOCK

[1]

A clock is getting ready to strike forever o'clock.
I do not know where the clock is, but it is somewhere.

I know it is somewhere, for I can hear it trying to
                    make up its mind to strike.
Somewhere is the place where it is while it is trying to make up its mind.

The sound it makes trying to make up its mind is purely metaphysical.
The sound is one you hear in your bloodstream and not your ear.

You hear it the way a man tied to a post in the yard of the
                    State Penitentiary of Utah
Could hear the mind of the Deputy Warden getting ready to say, "Fire!"

You hear it the way you hear your wife's breathing back
                    in a dark room at home, when
You are away on a trip and wake up in some hotel bedroom and
                    do not know where you are and do not know
                    offhand whose breath you do hear
                    there beside you.

[2]

The clock is taking time to make up its mind and that is why I have time
To think of some things that are not important but simply are.

A little two-year-old Negro girl-baby, with hair tied up in spindly
                                    little tits with strings of red rag,
Sits in the red dust. Except for some kind of rag around her middle,
                        she is naked, and black as a ripe plum in the
                                            sunshine.

Behind the child is a gray board shack, and from the mud-chimney a
                                twist of blue smoke is motionless
                                against the blue sky.
The fields go on forever, and whatever had been planted there is not
                            there now. The drouth does not see
                            fit to stop even now.

The pin-oak in the yard has been dead for years. The boughs are
                                black stubs against the blue sky.
Nothing alive is here but the child and a dominecker hen, flattened
                            puff-belly down, under the non-shade
                            of the pin-oak.

Inside the gray feathers, the body of the hen pants with the heat.
The yellow beak of the hen is open, and the flattened
                            string-thin tongue looks black and dry
                            and sharp as a pin.

The naked child with plum-black skin is intensely occupied.
From a rusted tin snuff can in the right hand, the child pours red
                        dust over the spread fingers of the left hand
                        held out prone in the bright air.

✿

The child stares at the slow-falling red dust. Some red dust piles
                    precariously up on the back of the little black
                    fingers thrust out. Some does not.
The sun blazes down on the naked child in the mathematical center of the
                            world. The sky glitters like brass.

A beat-up old 1931 Studebaker, of a kind you are too young ever to have
                seen, has recently passed down the dirt road, and a plume
                        of red dust now trails it
                        toward the horizon.
I watch the car that I know I am the man driving as it recedes into
                        distance and approaches the horizon.

[3]
I have now put on record one thing that is not important but simply is.
I watch the beat-up old green Studebaker moving like a dot into
                        distance trailing its red plume of
                        dust toward the horizon.

I wonder if it will ever get there. The wondering throbs like a
                                bruise inside my head.
Perhaps it throbs because I do not want to know the answer to my wondering.

The sun blazes down from the high center of the perfect concavity
                                of sky. The sky glitters like brass.
A clock somewhere is trying to make up its mind to strike forever o'clock.

X ∽

RATTLESNAKE COUNTRY

For James Dickey

1.

Arid that country and high, anger of sun on the mountains, but
One little patch of cool lawn:

Trucks

Had brought in rich loam. Stonework
Held it in place like a shelf, at one side backed
By the length of the house porch, at one end
By rock-fall. Above that, the mesquite, wolf-waiting. Its turn
Will, again, come.

Meanwhile, wicker chairs, all day,
Follow the shimmering shade of the lone cottonwood, the way that
Time, sadly seeking to know its own nature, follows
The shadow on a sun-dial. All day,
The sprinkler ejects its misty rainbow.

All day,

The sky shivers white with heat, the lake,
For its fifteen miles of distance, stretches
Tight under the white sky. It is stretched
Tight as a mystic drumhead. It glitters like neurosis.
You think it may scream, but nothing

Happens. Except that, bit by bit, the mountains
Get heavier all afternoon.

One day,
When some secret, high drift of air comes eastward over the lake,
Ash, gray, sifts minutely down on
Our lunch-time ice cream. Which is vanilla, and white.

There is a forest fire on Mount Ti-Po-Ki, which
Is at the western end of the lake there.

2.

If, after lunch, at God's hottest hour,
You make love, flesh, in that sweat-drench,
Slides on flesh slicker than grease. To grip
Is difficult.

At drink-time,
The sun, over Ti-Po-Ki, sets
Lopsided, and redder than blood or bruised cinnabar, because of
The smoke there. Later,
If there is no moon, you can see the red eyes of fire
Wink at you from
The black mass that is the mountain.

At night, in the dark room, not able to sleep, you
May think of the red eyes of fire that
Are winking from blackness. You may,
As I once did, rise up and go from the house. But,
When I got out, the moon had emerged from cloud, and I
Entered the lake. Swam miles out,
Toward the moonset. Motionless,
Awash, metaphysically undone in that silvered and
Unbreathing medium, and beyond
Prayer or desire, saw
The moon, slow, swag down, like an old woman's belly.

Going back to the house, I gave the now-dark lawn a wide berth.

At night the rattlers come out from the rock-fall.
They lie on the damp grass for coolness.

3.

I-yee!—

      and the wranglers, they cry on the mountain, and waking
At dawn-streak, I hear it.

            High on the mountain
I hear it, for snow-water there, snow long gone, yet seeps down
To green the raw edges and enclaves of forest
With a thin pasturage. The wranglers
Are driving our horses down, long before daylight, plunging
Through gloom of the pines, and in their joy
Cry out:

      I-yee!

         We ride this morning, and,
Now fumbling in shadow for *levis*, pulling my boots on, I hear
That thin cry of joy from the mountain, and what I have,
Literally, seen, I now in my mind see, as I
Will, years later, in my mind, see it—the horsemen
Plunge through the pine-gloom, leaping
The deadfall—*I-yee!—*
Leaping the boulder—*I-yee!—*and their faces
Flee flickering white through the shadow—*I-yee!—*
And before them,
Down the trail and in dimness, the riderless horses,
Like quicksilver spilled in dark glimmer and roil, go
Pouring downward.

        The wranglers cry out.

            And nearer.

✿

But,

Before I go for my quick coffee-scald and to the corral,
I hear, much nearer, not far from my open window, a croupy
Gargle of laughter.

It is Laughing Boy.

4.

Laughing Boy is the name that my host—and friend—gives his yard-hand.
Laughing Boy is Indian, or half, and has a hare-lip.
Sometimes, before words come, he utters a sound like croupy laughter.
When he utters that sound his face twists. Hence the name.

Laughing Boy wakes up at dawn, for somebody
Has to make sure the rattlers are gone before
The nurse brings my host's twin baby daughters out to the lawn. Laughing Boy,
Who does not like rattlers, keeps a tin can
Of gasoline covered with a saucer on an outer ledge of the porch.
Big kitchen matches are in the saucer. This
At the porch-end toward the rock-fall.

The idea is: Sneak soft-foot round the porch-end,
There between rattlers and rock-fall, and as one whips past,
Douse him. This with the left hand, and
At the same instant, with the nail of the right thumb,
Snap a match alight.

              The flame,
If timing is good, should, just as he makes his rock-hole,
Hit him.

The flame makes a sudden, soft, gaspy sound at
The hole-mouth, then dances there. The flame
Is spectral in sunlight, but flickers blue at its raw edge.

Laughing Boy has beautiful coordination, and sometimes
He gets a rattler. You are sure if
The soft, gasping sound and pale flame come before
The stub-buttoned tail has disappeared.

✿

Whenever
Laughing Boy really gets a rattler, he makes that sound like
Croupy laughter. His face twists.

Once I get one myself. I see, actually, the stub-buttoned tail
Whip through pale flame down into earth-darkness.

"The son-of-a-bitch," I am yelling, "did you see me, I got him!"

I have gotten that stub-tailed son-of-a-bitch.

I look up at the sky. Already, that early, the sky shivers with whiteness.

5.

What was *is* is now *was*. But
Is *was* but a word for wisdom, its price? Some from
That long-lost summer are dead now, two of the girls then young,
Now after their pain and delusions, worthy endeavors and lies, are,
Long since, dead.

The third
Committed her first adultery the next year, her first lover
A creature odd for her choosing, he who
Liked poetry and had no ambition, and
She cried out in his arms, a new experience for her. But
There were the twins, and she had, of course,
Grown accustomed to money.

Her second,
A man of high social position, who kept a score-card. With her,
Not from passion this time, just snobbery. After that,
From boredom. Forgot, finally,
The whole business, took up horse-breeding, which
Filled her time and even, I heard, made unneeded money, and in
The old news photo I see her putting her mount to the jump.
Her yet beautiful figure is poised forward, bent elbows
Neat to her tight waist, face
Thrust into the cleansing wind of her passage, the face
Yet smooth as a girl's, no doubt from the scalpel
Of the plastic surgeon as well as
From her essential incapacity
For experience.

The husband, my friend,
Would, by this time, be totally cynical. The children

Have been a disappointment. He would have heavy jowls.
Perhaps he is, by this time, dead.

As for Laughing Boy, he wound up in the pen. Twenty years.
This for murder. Indians
Just ought to leave whiskey to the white folks.

I can't remember the names of the others who came there,
The casual weekend-ers. But remember

What I remember, but do not
Know what it all means, unless the meaning inheres in
The compulsion to try to convert what now is *was*
Back into what was *is*.

     I remember
The need to enter the night-lake and swim out toward
The distant moonset. Remember
The blue-tattered flick of white flame at the rock-hole
In the instant before I lifted up
My eyes to the high sky that shivered in its hot whiteness.

And sometimes—usually at dawn—I remember the cry on the mountain.

All I can do is to offer my testimony.

XI ∽

HOMAGE TO THEODORE DREISER

On the Centennial of his Birth
(August 27, 1871)

> *Oh, the moon shines fair tonight along the Wabash,*
> *From the fields there comes the breath of new mown hay.*
> *Thro' the sycamores the candle lights are gleaming,*
> *On the banks of the Wabash, far away.*

> The Refrain of "On the Banks of the Wabash, Far Away"
> Words by Theodore Dreiser and Paul Dresser
> Music by Paul Dresser

1. PSYCHOLOGICAL PROFILE

Who is the ugly one slump-slopping down the street?
Who is the chinless wonder with the potato-nose?
Can't you hear the soft *plop* of the pancake-shaped feet?

He floats, like Anchises' son, in the cloud of his fine new clothes,
Safe, safe at last, from the street's sneer, toward a queen who will fulfill
The fate devised him by Venus—but where, oh when! That
                                              is what he never knows.

Born with one hand in his pants and one in the till,
He knows that the filth of self, to be loved, must be clad in glory,
So once stole twenty-five dollars to buy a new coat, and that is why still

The left eye keeps squinting backward—yes, history
Is gum-shoeing closer behind, with the constable-hand that clutches.
Watch his mouth, how it moves without sound, he is telling
                                              himself his own old story.

Full of screaming his soul is, and a stench like live flesh that scorches.
It's the screaming, and stench, of a horse-barn aflame,
And the great beasts rear and utter, their manes flare up like torches.

❂

From lies, masturbation, vainglory, and shame,
He moves in his dream of ladies swan-necked, with asses ample and sweet,
But knows that no kiss heals his soul, it is always the same.

The same—but a brass band plays in the distance, and the midnight cricket,
Though thinly, asseverates his name. He seeks amid the day's traffic a sign—
Some horseshoe or hunchback or pin—that now, at last, at the end of this street

He will enter upon his reality: but enters only in-
To your gut, or your head, or your heart, to enhouse there and stay,
And in that hot darkness lie lolling and swell—like a tumor, perhaps benign.

May I present Mr. Dreiser? He will write a great novel, someday.

2. Vital Statistics

[A]

Past Terre Haute, the diesels pound,
Eastward, westward, and under the highway slab the ground,
Like jello, shakes. Deep
In the infatuate and foetal dark, beneath
The unspecifiable weight of the great
Mid-America loam-sheet, the impacted
Particular particles of loam, blind,
Minutely grind.

At that depth and with that weight,
The particles, however minutely, vibrate
At the incessant passage
Of the transcontinental truck freight,
And concerning that emperor whose gut was god, Tacitus
Wrote, "ex urbe atque Italia inritamenta gulae gestabantur . . . ,"
And from both
Adriatic and Tyrrhenian seas, sea-crayfish and bivalve and,
Glare-eyed, the mullet, redder than flame,
Surrendered themselves in delight
To soothe that soft gullet wheredown all honor and empire
Slid slick, and wheels all night
Hummed on the highways to guarantee prompt delivery.

Saliva gathers in the hot darkness of mouth-tissue. The mouth,
Slack, drools at the corners, but ever so little.

                                        All night,
Past Terre Haute, tires, on the concrete, scream, and in that town,
Long before the age of the internal combustion engine, but not
Before that of gewgaw, gilt, and grab, when the war
For freedom had just given place to the war for the dollar,

Theodore Dreiser was born. That was on South Ninth Street, but
The exact address is, of course, lost. He was born
Into the vast anonymity of the poor.

                              Have you ever
Seen moonlight on the Wabash, far away?

[B]
On the wrong side of the tracks—that was where
He was born, and he never let you forget it, and his sisters
Had hot crotches and round heels.
He knew the gnaw of hunger, and how the first wind of winter feels,
He was born into the age of conspicuous consumption, and knew
How the heart, in longing, numbly congeals.

Nothing could help nothing, not reading Veblen or even Freud, for
The world is a great ass propped high on pillows, the cunt
Winks.

        Dreiser,
However, could not feel himself worthy. Not,
At least, of love. His nails,
Most horribly, were bitten. At night,
Sometimes, he wept. The bed springs
Creaked with the shift of his body, which,
In the Age of Faith and of Contempt of the World,
Would have been called a sack
Of stercorry: i.e., that matter the body ejects.

Sometimes he wept for the general human condition,
But he was hell on women.

＊

He had never loved any woman, he confessed,
Except his mother, whose broken shoes, he,
In childhood, had once caressed,
In the discovery of pity.

              Have you ever
Seen midnight moonlight on the Wabash,
While the diesel rigs boom by?
Have you ever thought how the moonlit continent
Would look from the tearless and unblinking distance of God's wide eye?

3. MORAL ASSESSMENT

You need call no psychiatrist
To anatomize his pain.
He suffers but the pain all men
Suffer in their human kind.
No—suffers, too,
His nobility of mind.

He denies it, he sneers at it,
In his icy nightmare of
The superlative of self;
Tries to, but cannot theorize past
The knowledge that
Others suffer, too, at last.

He is no philosopher.
His only gift is to enact
All that his deepest self abhors,
And learn, in his self-contemptive distress,
The secret worth
Of all our human worthlessness.

FLAUBERT IN EGYPT

For Dorothea Tanning

Winterlong, off La Manche, wind leaning. Gray stones of the gray
    city sluiced by gray rain. And he dreamed

Of desert and distance, sunlight like murder, lust and new colors whose
    names exploded the spectrum like dynamite,
    or cancer. So went there,

Who did not know what he was, or could be, though hoping he might
    find there his fate. Found
    what he found: with head shaven,

One lock at the occiput left, red tarboosh wind-flaunted, rode hard at
    the Sphinx, at the "Father of Terrors," which,
    in that perspective and distance, lifted slow from
    the desert, like a great ship from hull-down.
    At its height,
    it swung. His cry burst forth.

In the white-washed room, by the light of wicks in three oil-glasses and to
    the merciless *screak* of the rebec, with musicians
    blind-folded, the dancer, her breasts

cruelly bound to bulge upward and bare, above
    pink trousers flesh rippling in bronze, danced
    the dance which

He recalls from the oldest Greek vases—the leap on one foot with
    the free foot crossed over, the fingers
    aquiver, face calm, and
    slow centuries sifting like shadow. Light
    flickers on whitewash. He finds
    the *mons veneris* shaven, arse noble.
    That night three *coups*, and once
    performs cunnilingus. Fingers clutching her necklace,
    he lies. He remembers his boyhood. Her fingers
    and naked thighs twitch in sleep.

By day, on the minaret-top, the stork clacked its beak. At the edge of
    the carrion-field, the wild dog,
    snout blue from old blood,
    skulked, and camel bells in the distance.
    On the voyage down-Nile, on the slave-boat, old women,
    black and slaves too, who had seen all of life, tried
    to persuade the young girls, market-bound,
    to smile. But once,

On the height of Gebel Abusir, looking down on the Cataract, where
    the Nile flung itself to white froth on black granite, he
    cried out: "Eureka—the name, it is Emma!"
    And added: "Bovary." Pronouncing the *o*,
    as recorded by his companion, quite short.

❋

So home, and left Egypt, which was: palms black, sky red, and the river
    like molten steel, and the child's hand
    plucking his sleeve—"*Baksheesh*,
    and I'll get you my mother to fuck"—and the bath-boy
    he buggared, this in a clinical spirit and as
    a tribute to the host-country. And the chancre, of course,
    bright as a jewel on his member, and borne
    home like a trophy.

But not to be omitted: on the river at Thebes, having long stared
    at the indigo mountains of sunset, he let
    eyes fix on the motion of three wave-crests that,
    in unison, bowed beneath the wind, and his heart
    burst with a solemn thanksgiving to God for
    the fact he could perceive the worth of the
    world with such joy.

Years later, death near, he remembered the palm fronds—
    how black against a bright sky!

INTERJECTION #5:
SOLIPSISM AND THEOLOGY

Wild with ego, wild with world-blame,
He stared at the up-heave and enormity of ocean.
He said: *It does not even know my name.*

Wild with ego, wild with grief,
He stared at the antic small aphid green on the green leaf.
He said: *It has a home, but I—I'm the lost one.*

Wild with ego, wild with despair,
He stared at the icy and paranoid glitter of winter stars.
He said: *They would grind me like grain, small as dust, and not care.*

Wild with ego, wild with weeping,
He stared at the classic shut eyelids of his true love sleeping.
He said: *She sleeps, and the wild boar gashes my groin.*

Wild with ego, wild with wrong,
He stared into the dark pit of self whence all had sprung.
He said: *What is man that I should be mindful of him!*

But was—he was—and even yearned after virtue.

XIII ⌒
THE TRUE NATURE OF TIME

1. THE FARING

Once over water, to you borne brightly,
Wind off the North Sea cold but
Heat-streaked with summer and honed by the dazzle
Of sun, and the Channel boat banging
The chop like a shire-horse on cobbles—thus I,
Riding the spume-flash, by gull cries ringed,
Came.

Came, and the harbor slid smooth like an oil-slick.
It was the gray city, but the gray roof-slates
Sang blue in the sun, and the sea-cliffs,
Eastward, swung in that blue wind. I came thus,
And I, unseen, saw. Saw
You,

And you, at the pier edge, face lifting seaward
And toward that abstract of distance that I
Yet was and felt myself to be, stood. Wind
Tugged your hair. It tangled that brightness. Over
Your breast wind tautened the blue cloth, your skirt
Whipped, your bare legs were brown. Steel
Rang on steel. Shouts

Rose in that language.
Later,

The quiet place. Roses. Yellow. We came there, wind
Down now, sea slopping the rocks, slow, sun low and
Sea graying, but roses were yellow, climbing
The wall, it was stone. The last light
Came gilding a track across the gray water from westward.
It came leveling in to finger the roses. One
Petal, yellow, fell, slow.

At the foot of the gray stone, like light, it lay.
High beyond roses, a gull, in the last light, hung.

The sea kept slopping the rocks, slow.

2. THE ENCLAVE

Out of the silence, the saying. Into
The silence, the said. Thus
Silence, in timelessness, gives forth
Time, and receives it again, and I lie

In darkness and hear the wind off the sea heave.
Off the sea, it uncoils. Landward, it leans,
And at the first cock-crow, snatches that cry
From the cock's throat, the cry,
In the dark, like gold blood flung, is scattered. How

May I know the true nature of Time, if
Deep now in darkness that glittering enclave
I dream, hangs? It shines. Another
Wind blows there, the sea-cliffs,
Far in that blue wind, swing. Wind

Lifts the brightening of hair.

XIV ∽
VISION UNDER THE OCTOBER
MOUNTAIN: A LOVE POEM

Golding from green, gorgeous the mountain
high hangs in gold air, how
can stone float, it is

the image of authority, of reality—or, is it?—floating
with no weight, and glows, did we
once in the womb dream, dream
a gold mountain in gold
air floating, we in the

pulse and warm slosh of
that unbreathing bouillon, lulled in
the sway of that sweet
syllogism—oh, unambiguous—swung
in the tide of that bliss unbreathed, bathed in
un-self which was self, did we
dream a gold mountain, did
it glow in that faceless unfatuous
dark, did
it glow in gold air in the airless
abstraction of dark, floating high
above our blind eyes with

❀

no lashes yet, unbrined by grief yet, we
seeing nothing, but
what did we dream—a
gold mountain,
floating?

I want to understand the miracle
of your presence here by my side, your
gaze on the mountain. I want

to hear the whole story of how
you came here, with
particular emphasis on the development of

the human scheme of values.

XV ∽
STARGAZING

The stars are only a backdrop for
The human condition, the stars
Are brilliant above the black spruces,
And fall comes on. Wind

Does not move in the star-stillness, wind
Is afraid of itself, as you have been afraid in
Those moments when destruction and revelation
Have spat at each other like cats, and the mirror
Showed no breath, ha, ha, and the wind,

Far off in arctic starlight, is afraid
To breathe, and waits, huddled in
Sparse blackness of spruces, black glitter in starlight, in
A land, north, where snow already is, and waits:

And the girl is saying, "You do not look
At the stars," for I did not look at
The stars, for I know they are there, know
That if I look at the stars, I

Will have to live over again all I have lived
In the years I looked at stars and

Cried out, "O reality!" The stars
Love me. I love them. I wish they

Loved God, too. I truly wish that.

INTERJECTION #6:
WHAT YOU SOMETIMES FEEL ON
YOUR FACE AT NIGHT

Out of mist, God's
Blind hand gropes to find
Your face. The fingers
Want to memorize your face. The fingers
Will be wet with the tears of your eyes. God

Wants only to love you, perhaps.

XVI ∽
NEWS PHOTO

*(Of Man Coming Down Steps of Court House
after Acquittal on Charge of Having Shot
to Death an Episcopal Minister Reported
to Be Working Up the Niggers)*

[1]
Easy, easy, watch that belly!
Easy—and he lets it down
carefully, not that it is more than
the simple sag of middle age, but

now he knows how precious flesh is,
having with his own hand—finger,
rather—pump gun, finger on trigger of—*wham-mo!
oh, wham-mo, oh boy*—burst
flesh, not his own of course,
open and seen what spills
out, and so now buckles
the belt into flesh, his own, cruelly
in secret expiation perhaps, but also
to hold it preciously together, as you

can plainly see, for he wears no coat, autumn
being warm in Georgia—or is it
Alabama or Mississippi?—and
carries it, the belly, carefully down

the stairs, and descending, lets it
down carefully, step

to step down, like an armful of
crockery, the steps
blind. And his face—

he carries his face down
like, say, a large glass jar full
past brim, by bulge of surface tension, of
a fluid that looks like slightly murky ditch-water, but
can't be that, for obviously it
is too precious to risk spilling
even a single drop of. His
eyes turn inward. He

is innocent, they say
he is innocent, the law
says it too, so why

isn't he happy?

[2]
I wish he were happy, for
so few people manage it, and he
was not working for happiness
for himself, only for

the good of his country, so why
isn't he happy, why
does his tongue taste like an old sock, when
he hasn't had a drink for a week, and

is innocent, for they all say so, for
one bastard had a knife and it was six feet long, and

the other bastard had a French .75
from World War One he stole
off the lawn of the Court House
and was waving it over his head like
a cap pistol, and both

these nigger-loving bastards coming at him, and they
was disguised like preachers but they
was Comminists, and if they was preachers, they
was not Baptists nor even Methodist
preachers, and sure-God not no
Church of Christ preachers, and it was
the Jews and the Romans had Him hung,
them Romans being Roman Catholics, like the song says.

They nailed Him up, the bastards, and He bled for us all.

[3]
I wish he were happy, I
wish everybody were happy, the dead,
they are happy—*wham-mo!* and
you get happy right away—but

coming down the Court House steps, he
is not happy. Nothing
is like he had expected, as now he
moves toward the flash bulbs, his eyes
inward on innocence. But the eyes
of his wife, above him, to the left,
stare out at the flash bulbs in
outrage, for she hates the world. The son,

twelve years old,
is by the father's side.

It really is a family picture, even if

from higher up the stairs, friends,
admirers, and well-wishers crane
their heads to horn in
on the act and get in the paper, and
they really deserve to,
even if some are not such close friends, for

they have committed heroism in their hearts.

[4]
This, as he somehow knows, will come later:

> *Now I tell you, son, I don't care*
> *if niggers in new Buicks gets thicker in Morfee County than*
> *blue-bottle flies round buttermilk, and*
> *if ever nigger south of Mason and Dixon gets bleached till*
> *he's whiter'n a snowfall on the head of a albino old enough*
> *to be drawing Social Security for forty years, and*
> *if ever nigger in this State gets one of them No-Bull*
> *Prizes, which is what they call them Bull-Shit*
> *Prizes, which is what them square-heads in Sweden*
> *gives niggers, but as for me and what I done I know*
> *I done right in my heart and in the eyes of God-a-Mighty,*
> *my only regret being this durn preacher I'm referring to was not*
> *black, even if he wasn't no preacher in the first place,*
> *and now you are nigh grown up and off to*
> *college—now State is a fine place, but I want you to promise me*

you won't listen to a single word none of them perfessers
is gonna say against your raising, and not even open
any durn book that says different. You promise?

Yes, sir.

Well, God-damnit, get that look out of
your eyes when you look at me, before I
knock it out!—oh, son, oh, son,
you know I love you, don't you know it, son?

Yes. Yes, sir.

[5]
But now is now, and not later, and nothing
is what he had expected, for where
is the music, where
the flowers, the throwing of blossoms, the
flowing of banners, the black sedan and the gunning
of motorcycles as the State Troopers,
sun on white helmets, wheel
into formation for the escort, and where—yes, where—
is that pure calm of heart he had always longed for?

Yes, where is the kiss of his mother?

And where's the Governor? You'd think
that bastard might show some gratitude after
voting for him and doing all he had done, you'd think
he at least might send the Chief of the Highway Patrol.

✿

But look!—and why should he give a damn now
if some half-ass Governor never comes, for
look!—and it's Robert E. Lee, and—

    —yeah, look, and he's wearing
    his gray suit and a gray hat to match, and a
    sword round his waist, and he's waiting
    for me—yeah, for me!—and he's smiling, it must
    be a smile, even if I can't see his face good.
    Yeah, look! and he's lifting his hand up to take
    his hat off—yeah, Jesus!—his hat
    off to me—yeah—

                        —and lifting the hat off, he exposes
the skull to which skin with some hair,
gray, sparsely clings yet, as does
some leathery skin to face-bone, and gray hairs,
sparse too, to chin, and the chin-bone
drops wide open, and the sound
that comes out must be laughter, and Robert

E. Lee is laughing in sunshine, and half
across the state every pine needle
on that side of every pine tree
shrivels up as though hit by a blow torch, and
off in Jackson, Mississippi, or maybe
Montgomery, Alabama, the white paint on
the State House—it pops up and blisters, for Robert

E. Lee, he's laughing, he
shakes all over with laughing, he
rattles like a crap game on a tin roof, he

is laughing fit to kill, or would be
if he weren't dead already. But

there are tears in his eyes, or
at least would be, if
he had any.

Any eyes, I mean.

XVII〜
LITTLE BOY AND LOST SHOE

The little boy lost his shoe in the field.
Home he hobbled, not caring, with a stick whipping goldenrod.
Go find that shoe—I mean it, right now!
And he went, not now singing, and the field was big.

Under the sky he walked and the sky was big.
Sunlight touched the goldenrod, and yellowed his hair,
But the sun was low now, and oh, he should know
He must hurry to find that shoe, or the sun will be down.

Oh, hurry, boy, for the grass will be tall as a tree.
Hurry, for the moon has bled, but not like a heart, in pity.
Hurry, for time is money and the sun is low.
Yes, damn it, hurry, for shoes cost money, you know.

I don't know why you dawdle and do not hurry.
The mountains are leaning their heads together to watch.
How dilatory can a boy be, I ask you?

                                    Off in Wyoming,
The mountains lean. They watch. They know.

XVIII ∽
COMPOSITION IN GOLD AND RED-GOLD

Between the event and the word, golden
The sunlight falls, between
The brown brook's braiding and the mountain it
Falls, in pitiless plenitude, and every leaf
On the ruined apple tree is gold, and the apples all
Gold, too, especially those

On the ground. The gold of apples
That have fallen flushes to flame, but
Gold is the flame. Gold
Goes red-gold—and the scene:

A chipmunk is under the apple tree, sits up
Among gold apples, is
Golden in gold light. The chipmunk
Wriggles its small black nose
In the still center of the world of light.

The hair of the little girl is as brown-gold as
Brook water braiding in sunlight.

The cat, crouching by the gray stone, is gold, too.
The tail of the cat, half-Persian, weaves from side to side,

In infinite luxury, gold plume
Of sea-weed in that tide of light.
That is a motion that puts
The world to sleep.

The eyes of the cat are gold, and

I want to sleep. But
The event: the tiny
Shriek unstitches the afternoon, the girl
Screams, the sky
Tingles crystalline like a struck wine glass, and you
Feel the salt thickening, like grit, in your secret blood. Afterward

There is a difference in the quality of silence.
Every leaf, gold, hangs motionless on the tree, but
There is a difference in the quality of
Motionlessness: unverbed, unverved, they
Hang. On the last day will the sun
Explode? Or simply get too tired?

The chipmunk lies gold among the apples.
It is prone and totally relaxed like ripe
Fruit fallen, and,
Upon closer inspection, you can see
The faint smear of flame-gold at the base
Of the skull. This effect
Completes the composition.

The little girl
Holds the cat in her arms,
Crooning, "Baby, oh, baby." She weeps under
The powerful flood of gold light.

*

Somewhere, in the shade of alders, a trout
Hangs steady, head against a current like ice.

The eagle I had earlier seen climbing
The light tall above the mountain is

Now beyond sight.

INTERJECTION #7:
REMARKS OF SOUL TO BODY
(On the Occasion of a Birthday Party)

For Sergio and Alberta Perosa

You've toughed it out pretty well, old Body, done
Your duty, and gratified most of my whims, to boot—
Though sometimes, no doubt, against your better judgment,
Or even mine—and are still
Revving over satisfactorily, considering.

Keep doing your duty, yes, and some fine day
You'll get full pension, with your every need
Taken care of, and not a dime out of your own pocket—
Or anybody's pocket, for that matter—for you won't have
Any needs, not with the rent paid up in perpetuity.

But now tonight, to recognize your faithful service,
We've asked a few friends in, with their Bodies, of course—
Many of those Bodies quite charming, in fact—and after
You've drunk and dined, then you and all the other Bodies
Can go for a starlit romp, with the dogs, in the back pasture.

And we, the Owners—of Bodies, not dogs, I mean—
We'll sit by the fire and talk things over, remark
The baroque ironies of Time, exchange
Some childhood anecdotes, then on to the usual topics,
The death of the novel, the plight of democracy, and naturally, Vietnam.

✿

But let us note, too, how glory, like gasoline spilled
On the cement in a garage, may flare, of a sudden, up,

In a blinding blaze, from the filth of the world's floor.

XIX ～
THERE'S A GRANDFATHER'S CLOCK
IN THE HALL

There's a grandfather's clock in the hall, watch it closely. The
                minute hand stands still, then it jumps, and
                    in between jumps there is no-Time,
And you are a child again watching the reflection of early
                morning sunlight on the ceiling above your bed,

Or perhaps you are fifteen feet under water and holding your breath as
                you struggle with a rock-snagged anchor, or holding
                    your breath just long enough for one more long,
                        slow thrust to make the orgasm really
                            intolerable,
Or you are wondering why you do not really give a damn, as they
                trundle you off to the operating room,

Or your mother is standing up to get married and is very pretty and
                excited and is a virgin, and your heart overflows, and
                    you watch her with tears in your eyes, or
She is the one in the hospital room and she is really dying.

They have taken out her false teeth, which are now in a
                tumbler on the bedside table, and you know that only
                    the undertaker will ever put them back in.
You stand there and wonder if you will ever have to wear false teeth.

✿

She is lying on her back, and God, is she ugly, and
With gum-flabby lips and each word a special problem, she is asking
                              if it is a new suit that you are wearing.

You say yes and hate her uremic guts, for she has no right to make you
                              hurt the way that question hurts.
You do not know why that question makes your heart hurt like
                              a kick in the scrotum,

For you do not yet know that the question, in its murderous triviality, is the
                              last thing she will ever say to you,
Nor know what baptism is occurring in a sod-roofed hut or hole on the now night—
              swept steppes of Asia, and a million mouths, like ruined
                    stars in darkness, make a rejoicing that howls
                              like wind, or wolves,

Nor do you know the truth, which is: *Seize the nettle of innocence in*
                    both your hands, for this is the only
                                   way, and every
Ulcer in love's lazaret may, like a dawn-stung gem, sing—or even
                    burst into whoops of, perhaps, holiness.

But, in any case, watch the clock closely. Hold your breath and wait.
Nothing happens, nothing happens, then suddenly, quick as a wink, and
                              slick as a mink's prick, Time
                              thrusts through the time
                              of no-Time.

XX〜
READING LATE AT NIGHT,
THERMOMETER FALLING

[1]
The radiator's last hiss and steam-clang done, he,
Under the bare hundred-watt bulb that glares
Like truth, blanket
Over knees, woolly gray bathrobe over shoulders, handkerchief
On great bald skull spread, glasses
Low on big nose, sits. The book
Is propped on the blanket.

Thus—
But only in my mind's eye now:

and there, in the merciless
Glitter of starlight, the fields, mile
On mile over the county, stretch out and are
Crusted with ice which, whitely,
Answers the glitter of stars.

The mercury
Falls, the night is windless, mindless, and long, and somewhere,
Deep in the blackness of woods, the tendons
Of a massive oak bough snap with the sound of a
Pistol-shot.

*

A beam,
Somewhere in the colding house where he sits,
Groans. But his eyes do not lift. Who,
Long back, had said to me:

"When I was young I felt like I
Had to try to understand how things are, before I died."

[2]
But lived long.

        Lived
Into that purity of being that may
Be had past all ambition and the frivolous hope, but who now
Lives only in my mind's eye,

        though I
Cannot see what book is propped there under that forever
Marching gaze—Hume's *History of England,* Roosevelt's
Winning of the West, a Greek reader,
Now Greek to him and held in his hands like a prayer, or
Some college text book, or Freud on dreams, abandoned
By one of the children. Or, even,
Coke or Blackstone, books forbidding and blackbound, and once I,
Perhaps twelve then, found an old photograph:

        a young man,
In black coat, high collar, and string tie, black, one hand out
To lie with authority on a big book (Coke or Blackstone?), eyes
Lifted into space.

    And into the future.

✿

                              Which
Had not been the future. For the future
Was only his voice that, now sudden, said:

"Son, give me that!"

He took it from my hand, said:

"Some kinds of foolishness a man is due to forget, son."

Tore it across. Tore
Time, and all that Time had been, across. Threw it
Into the fire. Who,
Years later, would say:

"I reckon I was lucky enough to learn early that a man
                    can be happy in his obligations."

Later, I found the poems. Not good.

[3]
The date on the photograph: 1890.

He was very young then. And poor.

Man lives by images. They
Lean at us from the world's wall, and Time's.

[4]
Night of the falling mercury, and ice-glitter.

Drouth-night of August and the horned insect booming
At the window-screen.

Ice-field, dusty road: distance flees.

And he sits there, and I think I hear
The faint click and grind of the brain as
It translates the perception of black marks on white paper into
Truth.

Truth is all.

We must love it.

And he loved it, who once said:

"It is terrible for a man to live and not know."

Every day he walked out to the cemetery to honor his dead.
That was truth, too.

[5]
Dear Father—Sir—the "Sir" being
The sometimes disturbed recollection
Of the time when you were big, and not dead, and I
Was little, and all boys, of that time and place, automatically
Said that to their fathers, and to any other grown man,
White of course, or damned well got their blocks
Knocked off.

✿

So, Sir, I,
Who certainly could never have addressed you on a matter
As important as this when you were not dead, now
Address you on it for the last time, even though
Not being, after all my previous and sometimes desperate efforts,
Sure what a son can ever say to a father, even
A dead one.

Indecipherable passion and compulsion—well,
Wouldn't it be sad to see them, of whatever
Dark root, dwindle into mere
Self-indulgence, habit, tic of the mind, or
The picking of a scab. Reality
Is hard enough to come by, but even
In its absence we need not blaspheme
It.

Not that
You ever could, God knows. Though I,
No doubt, have, and even now
Run the risk of doing so when I say
That I live in a profound, though
Painful, gratitude to you for what
You could not help but be: i.e., yourself.

Who, aged eighty, said:

"I've failed in a lot of things, but I don't think anybody
can say that I didn't have guts."

Correct.

✿

And I,
In spite of my own ignorance and failures,
Have forgiven you all your virtues.

Even your valor.

[6]
Who, aged eighty-six, fell to the floor,
Unconscious. Two days later,
Dead. Thus they discovered your precious secret:
A prostate big as a horse-apple. Cancer, of course.

No wonder you, who had not spent a day in bed,
Or uttered a single complaint, in the fifty years of my life,
Cried out at last.

You were entitled to that. It was only normal.

[7]
So disappeared.

Simply not there.

And the seasons,
Nerve-tingling heat or premonitory chill, swung
Through the year, the years swung,

and the past, great
Eater of dreams, secrets, and random data, and
Refrigerator of truth, moved

Down what green valley at a glacier's
Massive pace,

        moving
At a pace not to be calculated by the trivial sun, but by
A clock more unforgiving that, at
Its distance of mathematical nightmare,
Glows forever. The ice-mass, scabbed
By earth, boulders, and some strange vegetation, moves
So imperceptibly that it seems
Only more landscape.

        Until,
In late-leveling light, some lunkhead clodhopper,
The day's work done, now trudging home,
Stops.

    Stares.

       And there it is.

          It looms.

The bulk of the unnamable and de-timed beast is now visible,
Erect, in the thinly glimmering shadow of ice.

                The lunkhead
Stares.

    The beast,
From his preternatural height, unaware of
The cringe and jaw-dropped awe crouching there below, suddenly,
As if that shimmer of ice-screen had not even been there, lifts,

✻

Into distance,

the magisterial gaze.

[8]
The mercury falls. Tonight snow is predicted. This,
However, is another country.

XXI ∽
FOLLY ON ROYAL STREET
BEFORE THE RAW FACE OF GOD

Drunk, drunk, drunk, amid the blaze of noon,
Irrevocably drunk, total eclipse or,
At least, almost, and in New Orleans once,
In French Town, spring,
Off the Gulf, without storm warnings out,
Burst, like a hurricane of
Camellias, sperm, cat-squalls, fish-smells, and the old
Pain of fulfillment-that-is-not-fulfillment, so
Down Royal Street—Sunday and the street
Blank as my bank account
With two checks bounced—we—
C. and M. and I, every
Man-jack skunk-drunk—
Came.

　　A cat,
Gray from the purple shadow of bougainvillaea,
Fish-head in dainty jaw-clench,
Flowed fluid as thought, secret as sin, across
The street. Was gone. We,
In the shock of that sudden and glittering vacancy, rocked
On our heels.

✻

                    A cop,
Of brachycephalic head and garlic breath,
Toothpick from side of mouth and pants ass-bagged and holster low,
From eyes the color of old coffee grounds,
Regarded with imperfect sympathy
La condition humaine—
Which was sure-God what we were.

We rocked on our heels.

                    At sky-height—
Whiteness ablaze in dazzle and frazzle of light like
A match flame in noon-blaze—a gull
Kept screaming above the doomed city.
It screamed for justice against the face of God.

Raw-ringed with glory like an ulcer, God's
Raw face stared down.

                    And winked.

                              We
Mouthed out our Milton for magnificence.

For what is man without magnificence?

Delusion, delusion!

                    But let
Bells ring in all the churches.
Let likker, like philosophy, roar
In the skull. Passion

Is all. Even
The sleaziest.

　　　War
Came. Among the bed-sheet Arabs, C.
Sported his gold oak leaf. Survived.
Got back. Back to the bank. But
One morning was not there. His books,
However, were in apple-pie order. His suits,
All dark, hung in the dark closet. Drawn up
In military precision, his black shoes,
Though highly polished, gave forth
No gleam in that darkness. In Mexico,
He died.

　　　For M.,
Twenty years in the Navy. Retired,
He fishes. Long before dawn, the launch slides out.
Land lost, he cuts the engine. The launch
Lifts, falls, in the time of the sea's slow breath.
Eastward, first light is like
A knife-edge honed to steel-brightness
And laid to the horizon. Sometimes,
He comes back in with no line wet.

As for the third, the tale
Is short. But long,
How long the art, and wisdom slow!—for him who
Once rocked on his heels, hearing the gull scream,
And quoted Milton amid the blaze of noon.

INTERJECTION #8:
OR, SOMETIMES, NIGHT

For Paul Horgan

The unsleeping principle of delight that
Declares the arc of the apple's rondure; of, equally,
A girl's thigh that, as she lies, lifts
And draws full forward in its subtly reversed curve from
Buttock bulge to the now softly closing under-knee nook; and of
The flushed dawn cumulus: the principle
That brackets, too, the breaker's crest in one
Timeless instant, glittering, between
Last upward erg and, suddenly,
Totter and boom; and that,
In a startling burst of steel-brilliant sun, makes
The lone snow-flake dance—
                              this principle is what,
Intermittently at least and at unlikely moments,
Comes into my mind,
Whether by day or, sometimes, night.

XXII ∽

SUNSET WALK IN THAW-TIME IN VERMONT

1.

Rip, whoosh, wing-whistle: and out of
The spruce thicket, beating the snow from
Black spruce boughs, it
Bursts. The great partridge cock, black against flame-red,
Into the red sun of sunset, plunges. Is
Gone.

     In the ensuing
Silence, abrupt in
Back-flash and shiver of that sharp startlement, I
Stand. Stare. In mud-streaked snow,
My feet are. I,
Eyes fixed past black spruce boughs on the red west, hear,
In my chest, as from a dark cave of
No-Time, the heart
Beat.

    Where
Have the years gone?

2.

All day the stream, thaw-flooding, foamed down its gorge.
Now, skyless but for the high-tangled spruce night, it
Moves, and the bulge and slick twining of muscular water, foam-
Slashed and white-tettered, glints now only in
The cold, self-generating light of snow
Strong yet in the darkness of rock-banks.

                                                    The boulder
Groans in the stream, the stream heaves
In the deep certainty of its joy, like
Doom, and I,
Eyes fixed yet on the red west, begin to hear—though
Slow and numb as upon waking—
The sound of water that moves in darkness.

I stand, and in my imagination see
The slick heave of water, blacker than basalt, and on it
The stern glint, like steel, of snow-darkness.

3.

On the same spot in summer, at thrush-hour, I,
As the last light fails, have heard that full
Shadow-shimmered and deep-glinting liquidity, and
Again will; but not now.

Now
Here stare westward, and hear only
The movement of darkening water, and from
Whatever depth of being I am, ask
To be made worthy of my human failures and folly, and
Worthy of my human ignorance and anguish, and of
What soul-stillness may be achieved as I
Stand here with the cold exhalation of snow
Coiling high as my knees.

Meanwhile,
On the mountain's east hump, darkness coagulates, and
Already, where sun has not touched for hours, the new
Ice-crystal frames its massive geometry.

4.

When my son is an old man, and I have not,
For some fifty years, seen his face, and, if seeing it,
Would not even be able to guess what name it wore, what
Blessing should I ask for him?

That some time, in thaw-season, at dusk, standing
At woodside and staring
Red-westward, with the sound of moving water
In his ears, he
Should thus, in that future moment, bless,
Forward into that future's future,
An old man who, as he is mine, had once
Been his small son.

For what blessing may a man hope for but
An immortality in
The loving vigilance of death?

XXIII ∽
BIRTH OF LOVE

Season late, day late, sun just down, and the sky
Cold gunmetal but with a wash of live rose, and she,
From water the color of sky except where
Her motion has fractured it to shivering splinters of silver,
Rises. Stands on the raw grass. Against
The new-curdling night of spruces, nakedness
Glimmers and, at bosom and flank, drips
With fluent silver. The man,

Some ten strokes out, but now hanging
Motionless in the gunmetal water, feet
Cold with the coldness of depth, all
History dissolving from him, is
Nothing but an eye. Is an eye only. Sees

The body that is marked by his use, and Time's,
Rise, and in the abrupt and unsustaining element of air,
Sway, lean, grapple the pond-bank. Sees
How, with that posture of female awkwardness that is,
And is the stab of, suddenly perceived grace, breasts bulge down in
The pure curve of their weight and buttocks
Moon up and, in that swelling unity,
Are silver, and glimmer. Then

✿

The body is erect, she is herself, whatever
Self she may be, and with an end of the towel grasped in each hand,
Slowly draws it back and forth across back and buttocks, but
With face lifted toward the high sky, where
The over-wash of rose color now fails. Fails, though no star
Yet throbs there. The towel, forgotten,
Does not move now. The gaze
Remains fixed on the sky. The body,

Profiled against the darkness of spruces, seems
To draw to itself, and condense in its whiteness, what light
In the sky yet lingers or, from
The metallic and abstract severity of water, lifts. The body,
With the towel now trailing loose from one hand, is
A white stalk from which the face flowers gravely toward the high sky.
This moment is non-sequential and absolute, and admits
Of no definition, for it
Subsumes all other, and sequential, moments, by which
Definition might be possible. The woman,

Face yet raised, wraps,
With a motion as though standing in sleep,
The towel about her body, under the breasts, and,
Holding it there, hieratic as lost Egypt and erect,
Moves up the path that, stair-steep, winds
Into the clamber and tangle of growth. Beyond
The lattice of dusk-dripping leaves, whiteness
Dimly glimmers, goes. Glimmers and is gone, and the man,

Suspended in his darkling medium, stares
Upward where, though not visible, he knows
She moves, and in his heart he cries out that, if only
He had such strength, he would put his hand forth

And maintain it over her to guard, in all
Her out-goings and in-comings, from whatever
Inclemency of sky or slur of the world's weather
Might ever be. In his heart
He cries out. Above

Height of the spruce-night and heave of the far mountain, he sees
The first star pulse into being. It gleams there.

I do not know what promise it makes to him.

XXIV ∽
A PROBLEM IN SPATIAL COMPOSITION

[1]
Through the high window, upright rectangle of distance:

Over the green interstices and shambling glory, yet bright, of forest,
Distance flees westward, the sun low.

Beyond the distance of forest, hangs that which is blue:
Which is, in knowledge, a tall scarp of stone, gray, but now is,
In the truth of perception, stacked like a mass of blue cumulus.
Blue deepens.

　　　　What we know, we know, and
Sun now down, flame, above blue, dies upward forever in
Saffron: pure, pure and forever, the sky
Upward is. The lintel of the high window, by interruption,

Confirms what the heart knows: *beyond* is *forever*—

　　　　　　　　　　　　　　and nothing moves
Across the glister of saffron, and under the
Window the brook that,
After lalling and lounging daylong by shallow and reach,
Through dapple to glitter, now recessed in
Its premature leaf-night, utters a deeper-toned meditation.

[2]
While out of the green, up-shining ramshackle of leaf, set
In the lower right foreground, the stub
Of a great tree, gaunt-blasted and black, thrusts.

                                        A single
Arm jags upward, higher goes, and in that perspective, higher
Than even the dream-blue of distance that is
The mountain.

            Then
Stabs, black, at the infinite saffron of sky.

All is ready.

            The hawk,
Entering the composition at the upper left frame
Of the window, glides,
In the pellucid ease of thought and at
His breathless angle,
Down.

            Breaks speed.

                    Hangs with a slight lift and hover.

                                        Makes contact.

The hawk perches on the topmost, indicative tip of
The bough's sharp black and skinny jag skyward.

[3]
The hawk, in an eyeblink, is gone.

Robert Penn Warren was born in Guthrie, Kentucky, in 1905. After graduating *summa cum laude* from Vanderbilt University (1925), he received a master's degree from the University of California (1927), did graduate work at Yale University (1927–28) and then at Oxford as a Rhodes Scholar (B. Litt., 1930).

Mr. Warren has published many books, including nine novels, ten volumes of poetry, a volume of short stories, a play, a collection of critical essays, a biography, a historical essay, and two studies of race relations in America. This body of work has been published in a period of forty-four years—a period during which Mr. Warren has also had an active career as a professor of English.

All the King's Men (1946) was awarded the Pulitzer Prize for fiction. *Promises* (1957) won the Pulitzer Prize for poetry, the Edna St. Vincent Millay Prize of the Poetry Society of America, and the National Book Award. In 1944 Mr. Warren occupied the Chair of Poetry of the Library of Congress. In 1959 he was elected to the American Academy of Arts and Letters. In 1967 he received the Bollingen Prize in Poetry for *Selected Poems: New and Old, 1923–1966*, and in 1970 the National Medal for Literature. In 1974 he was chosen by the National Endowment for the Humanities to deliver the third Annual Jefferson Lecture in the Humanities.

Mr. Warren lives in Connecticut with his wife, Eleanor Clark (author of *Rome and a Villa, The Oysters of Locmariaquer* and *Baldur's Gate*), and their two children, Rosanna and Gabriel.

к

Wilmington Public Library

Wilmington, NC 28401